DOLLY HIT ME BACK!

by

Bil Keane

FAWCETT GOLD MEDAL • NEW YORK

"I don't know why Mommy and Daddy ever let you into this family!"

"Do I have to CLEAN UP my room, Mommy,
or can I just neaten it a little?"

"I'm teachin' PJ to write. What do we call this letter?"

"It's very clear and there aren't any clouds. Why can't we see God up there?"

"Look, Mommy! We're wading!"

"Wanna help us fly our kite, Daddy?"

"I love me, I love me not . . ."

"Could I eat this yesterday?".

"Oooooh! The wind is ticklin' my tummy!"

"An echo is like hearing yourself in a mirror."

"Why can't I get the new clothes sometime
and let Billy wear my hand-me-ups?"

"Do sharks ever come up in bathtubs?"

"Let's pretend I'm getting married and you guys sing 'Here Comes the Prize.'"

"I was bringin' these home for you, Mommy, but they melted."

"He's not here, but I'm the BOY of the house."

"Will you promise to be quiet if I take you tennising
with me?"

"In the wintertime I think ice cream men just turn into normal people."

"Birthday?"　　　　　　"September.23rd."
"What year?"　　　　　　"Every year."

"Mommy, at weddings, why do they say 'awful wedded wife'?"

"Could we have the meat in a doggy bag, and the fish in a kittycat bag and the lettuce in a turtle bag and . . ."

"Doesn't your camera have fine tuning, Daddy?"

"Let's go over there, Mommy! That lady's givin' out free examples!"

"Be patient, PJ. You can have my popcicle when I'm through."

"Mommy, Goldie won't grow up to be a shark, will she?"

"Stop that noise, PJ! I need a little piece of quiet around here!"

"No, thank you."

"Why don't eggs have a tab you can pull?"

"It's just the soap — we won't need that."

"Betcha I'd sleep later if I didn't have to take an afternoon nap."

"Mommy, why don't you 'God bless me' when I sneeze 'stead of sayin' 'Cover your mouth'?"

"Mommy's payin' me a quarter to do this. How much are you gettin'?"

"I'm teachin' PJ to swing, but he can't learn to get off by himself."

"Sam's heart's in the right place, though,
Daddy."

"If I put it under my pillow will the button fairy
bring me some money?"

"We didn't go to the seashore at all during the
summer 'cause my mom went
to see 'Jaws.'"

"Could I use some of your perfume, Mommy? I've got a big favor to ask Daddy."

"Don't we have any RED apples? These are still yel-
low."

"See? He rows himself with his tail."

"Dolly called me a 'walking 'saster area.' Is that good
or should I be mad?"

"Mommy likes to talk to her plants 'cause they never talk back."

"I picked it out — Mommy just paid for it."

"Daddy's shining his shoes with PJ!"

"My daddy said 'Is he here again?' and Mommy thinks you charge too much."

"If there wasn't so much JUNK in this drawer, I might be able to find the other half of my yo-yo."

"If you want me I'll be at Alan's or Scott's or
Mark's or Todd's or Joey's."

"I can't take this note to my teacher, Mommy. You didn't leave enough margin."

"It was a pretty good party, 'cept there were GIRLS there."

"Daddies believe 'zactly what you say but mommies can read your mind."

"Which side of the toast do I butter?"

"Here you go, Mommy — I found you some hangers!"

"You sound tired, dear. Why don't you take a nap?"

"Mommy, will you light these so I can start practicing for my birthday?"

"Kittycats only hear what they wanna hear, Jeffy."

"Do you want some peaches?" "No."
"No what?" "No peaches."

"The baby sitter last night said she'd never sit for us
again."

"When we come out of school the lifeguard helps us across the street."

"Daddy showed me how to cut out paper persons."

"Why didn't they finish that bridge, Daddy?"

"We're talking to Grandma in stereo!"

"We flipped a coin — I said heads, Jeffy said tails,
but it came up a building!"

"Hear that? Mommy says she's tired. Now we'll have to go to bed early."

"Grandma lets us help ourselves to as many as we want."

"The ones up front are the headlights. These are the footlights."

"I didn't do it, Mommy."

"Read slower, Daddy. I can't listen that fast."

"Okay, Scott, now hang up and let ME call YOU."

"Mommy, what year was PJ invented?"

"Will somebody deck up the cards so I can serve 'em?"

"Because you're not a suitcase, that's why."

"I'm just washin' off my apple."

"Pretty soon we'll find out what kind of a face he has."

"I'll trade you this year — I'LL take the children around to the houses and YOU stay home and answer the confounded doorbell."

"That's our daddy. He's dressed as himself."

"Mommy's asleep but I'll play cards with you till she wakes up."

"Guess somebody must've fooled Mother Nature again."

"When the guy on TV did it all the dishes stayed on the table!"

"Mommy! Jeffy's just holdin' his hands NEAR the water!"

"Do I HAFTA look like Daddy when I grow up?"

"Mommy! I can get an autographed football if
we just go down to DG Home Center
and buy a color TV!"

"I lost a card from this deck but it doesn't matter 'cause it was only a two."

"I have the queen. The one I need is her hus-
band."

"Know what Grandma wears on her gold chain? Her glasses."

"Why does Sam need a license? He doesn't go fishing or hunting or get married or drive a car or . . ."

"Did you get the pictures we sent, Grandma? . . . And the gift? . . ."

"Ooops! Mommy! It's It's the wrong Grandma!"

"When they gather into a group like that,
they're tellin' secrets!"

"Does it make any noise?"

"Aren't they goin' to have Thanksgiving this
year, Mommy?"

"How many stairs does this thing use up in a day?"

"All I'm gonna ask Santa for this year is a baby sister."

"There's nothing here for you."

"It costs too much for Mommy and Daddy to buy, but we'll ask Santa for it."

"Aw — it's another one marked 'Do Not Open Till Christmas.'"

" 'Twas the night before Christmas and all through the house,
Not a mouse was s---, not a --- the creatures were hung by the . . .
'Twas the night before Christmas and . . .'"

"The Lanes put THEIR lights around the front
door and all their windows, across the
roof, over the chimney and . . ."

"Why did you say 'Yes, Virginia, there is a Santa Claus'? My name's Dolly, not Virginia."

"... and I got a frisbee for Aunt Nancy and this harmonica for Grandma and ..."

"What do I want, Mommy?"

"An old fashioned Christmas means like they had back in the sixties."

"They aren't REAL carolers, Mommy—one of them is Linda's mother."

"Can God give messages to Santa Claus?"

"I bought everybody's present 'cept one.
What can I get for Daddy that costs
23 cents?"

"Mommy! That red Christmas light won't let
me go to sleep!"

"It's gettin' dark, Mommy! Guess we better get ready for bed before You-Know-Who comes!"

"Can we go outside and play with the boxes?"

"I'm goin' to bed early. I wanna be in good shape to work on that new jigsaw puzzle tomorrow."

"I guess it's just a little too much Christmas excitement."

"Boy, Grandma! I hope I can play with this and not have to wear it!"

"Already? Gee! We just put it UP!"

"Don't forget, Mommy! If we fall asleep, be
sure to wake us up at midnight!"

"Jeffy and PJ aren't startin' the New Year off right!"

"There's a different note in every hole."

"Is it anybody important?"

"I'm tryin' to remember, Mommy, but I can't think of it — what animal does meat loaf come from?"

"Wow! It's below nothing!"

"Watch out, Mommy! Don't step on the dragon!"

"Will you put my watch on so it's lookin' at me?"

"What would the little boy down the lane do
with a bag of wool?"

"Did you know your hair was changin' color
down near your head?"

"Which toe did you hurt?"
"My thumb toe."

"When he sleeps he takes his head indoors."

"Hi, Mommy! Hint, hint!"

"I have to catch up on my diary. What did I do on January 2nd, 3rd, 4th, 5th, 6th, 7th and 8th?"

"I'm playin' my organ lady records to make
your plant happy so it'll grow."

"Mommy, if the McCauleys bring permission slips, can they go skiing with us?"

"How many times have I told you not to talk
with your mouth full? Answer me!"